My Senses

TOUCHING

by Grace Jones

Words written in **yellow** are explained in the glossary on page 24.

Photocredits: Abbreviations: l-left, r-right, b-bottom, t-top, c-centre, m-middle.
All images are courtesy of Shutterstock.com.
Front Cover – CHAIWATPHOTOS. 2 – Africa Studio. 3 – mania-room. 4 – Zurijeta. 5 – Martin Valigursky. 6 – Dan loei tam loei.
7 – Velychko. 8tr – Nerthuz. 8 – Patrick Foto. 9 – AlikeYou. 10 – Purino. 11 – strelov. 12 – wckiw. 13 – Maria Uspenskaya. 14 –
Ventura. 15 – Boris Mrdja. 16 – Tom Wang. 17 – Ruslan Guzov. 18 – Sergey Nivens. 19 – Hurst Photo. 20 – Ljupco Smokovski. 21
– Alsu. 22tl – Zayats Svetlana. 22tr – Silberkorn. 22bl – Crepesoles. 22br – Joop Hoek. 23 – Syda Productions

CONTENTS

©2016
Book Life
King's Lynn
Norfolk PE30 4LS

ISBN: 978-1-910512-66-1

Written by:
Grace Jones
Edited by:
Gemma McMullen
Designed by:
Drue Rintoul

A catalogue record for this book
is available from the British Library.

WHAT ARE MY SENSES?

We all have 5 **senses**. They are sight, smell, taste, touch and hearing.

Your senses tell you what is going on around you.

HOW DO I FEEL TOUCH?

SKIN

You feel everything you touch through your skin.

You can feel things on any part of your body.

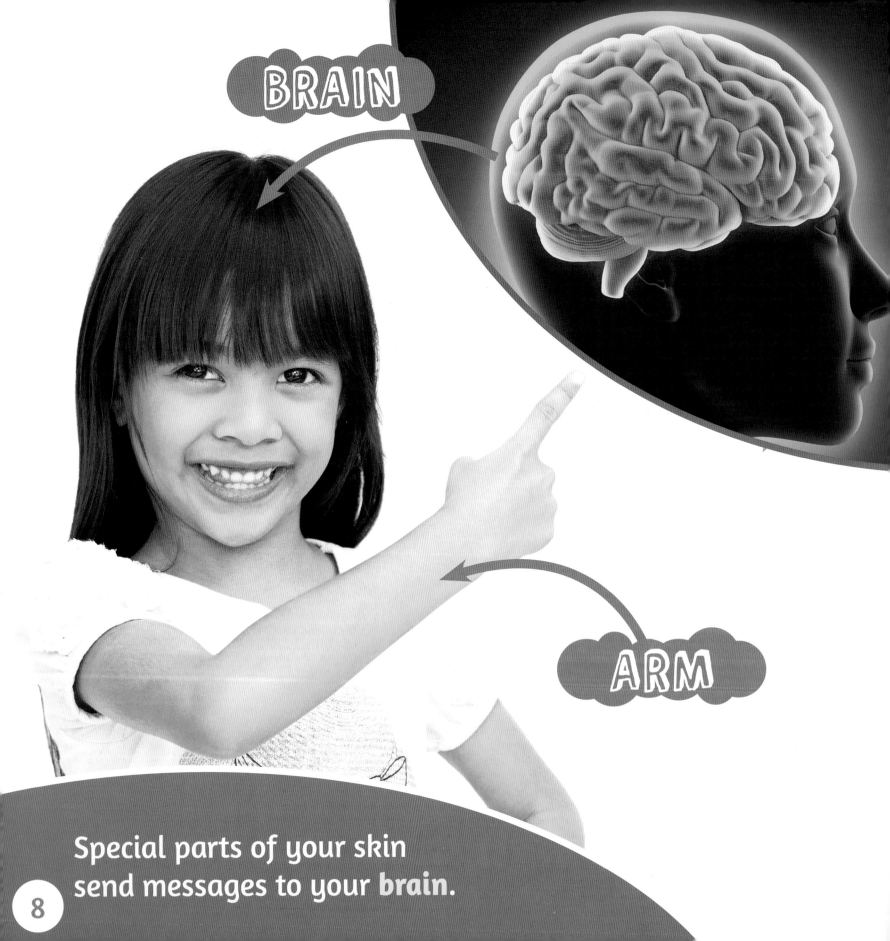

BRAIN

ARM

Special parts of your skin
send messages to your **brain**.

Your brain tells you what you are touching.

TOUCHING AND FEELING

How an object feels is called its texture.

Textures can be rough, smooth, soft or hard.

SOFT

A teddy bear feels soft when you touch it.

Some toys feel hard when you touch them.

HARD

AT THE SEASIDE

SMOOTH

ROUGH

Shells found on the beach can have smooth or rough textures.

A starfish feels rough when you touch it.

IN THE KITCHEN

ROUGH

Your sense of touch tells you when something is cold.

It also tells you when something is hot.

HOT

STAYING SAFE

Your sense of touch helps to keep you safe from danger.

When you feel something is too hot, you move away from it to stop your skin from **burning**.

SUPER SENSES!

People who are **blind** use their sense of touch to read.

They read by touching
bumps on the page.

WHAT CAN YOU SMELL?

With a partner, find four objects
with different textures. Tell your partner
to shut their eyes and let them touch each object.

Can they guess what each object is?
Ask them to describe how each one feels.

GLOSSARY

BLIND
someone who cannot see.

BRAIN
tells your body what to do.

BURNING
an injury caused by heat.

SENSES
tell you what is going
on around you.

INDEX